THE OXFORD OF INSPECTOR MORSE

CHIEF INSPECTOR MORSE died on television in front of millions in November 2000. Barely 15 months later actor John Thaw, who had made the curmudgeonly detective his own, died of cancer. Morse fans the world over mourned twice – once for the uncompromising detective, whose passions were solving crosswords, drinking real ale and listening to Wagner, and again for the actor who had breathed life into a detective who was already a bit of a dinosaur when he first appeared on our screens in 1987.

John Thaw and Colin Dexter

Many people already knew the character of Inspector Morse from the books of Oxford writer Colin Dexter, whose work was adapted for the screen. Dexter had his first 'Inspector Morse' novel, *Last Bus to Woodstock*, published in 1975. Six more were on bookshop shelves before the first television film, *The Dead of Jericho*, written by Anthony Minghella, was broadcast.

Morse stepped from the pages onto the screen with a less sleazy, but just as grumpy, image. Lewis, on the other hand, became a young sergeant (played by Kevin Whately), rather than the staid grandfather of the novels. Morse's beloved Lancia was scrapped and became his 1960 red 2.4 litre Jaguar Mark II, registration number 248 RPA. The instant success of the television series was recognized as a combination of terrific writing, well-spun plots and a cast of talented and well-known actors. But there was another crucial element to the Morse magic and that was its unrivalled setting – the historic city of Oxford.

Oxford, its colleges and ancient buildings, its alleyways and twisting streets, the mystery of the academic life, the often baffling university ceremonies and the bitter rivalries that beset those in authority at the colleges, are all understood by Morse, who we learn was once an undergraduate at St John's College. The settings – centuries-old gatehouses, college quads, halls and chapels, great spires, ancient cloisters, towers and rotundas – cannot be bettered and cannot be forgotten by millions of viewers, many of whom make pilgrimages to England's oldest university city to see the Oxford of Inspector Morse.

Use this guide to find your way to the colleges, streets, museums and public buildings that appeared in the television episodes and to follow in the footsteps of Britain's favourite detective.

John Thaw and Kevin Whately

MURDER IN THE COLLEGES

CHIEF INSPECTOR MORSE strides around Oxford, through college gatehouses, in and out of the Bodleian and the Ashmolean Museum, even into college libraries that are closed to lesser mortals, with the confidence born of a long acquaintance with the city and its iconic buildings. There are lingering shots of the great domed Radcliffe Camera, and the Old Schools Quadrangle with the statue of the Earl of Pembroke standing guard at one end and the Tower of the Five Orders at its Catte Street entrance. Morse fans see the 'Bridge of Sighs' and know exactly what it is – but it's not always so easy to work out which college is featured in a particular episode.

Filming in the grounds of Hertford College

You will read that the fictional Lonsdale College is Brasenose, and so it is – sometimes. In the *Settling of the Sun*, for example, a group of summer-school students is deposited outside Lonsdale College and indeed they walk through Brasenose gatehouse. But the dining halls of both Oriel College and Brasenose are used, and the dramatic confession of vengeful Mrs Warbut, Lonsdale's domestic bursar, takes place at the altar in the chapel of nearby Exeter College. Although Merton College is the setting for the fictional Beaufort College of *The Infernal Serpent*, the funeral scene is shot in Oriel College chapel and the final drama played out in University College chapel. As far as we, the viewers, are concerned the transition is seamless and Beaufort is just one college.

This guide is divided into different parts of Oxford, allowing you to explore the locations used in each area and see for yourself where the filming was done. On page 32 there is a list of colleges used as locations in the *Inspector Morse* episodes. Most of them are open to the public at certain times, so it is possible to see the reality behind the drama of Morse's Oxford.

Morse walking out of the Old Schools Quadrangle

OXFORD AFFAIRS

CHIEF INSPECTOR MORSE gives up his secrets slowly. It is not until he meets Adele Cecil (Judy Loe), his last love, that he reveals his first name, in *Death is Now My Neighbour*. He gives it obliquely – as a crossword clue – 'My whole life's effort has revolved around Eve.' Nine letters. She works it out. Endeavour. Morse tells her that this name suited the religious convictions of his Quaker mother and his father, passionate about Captain Cook and his ship, the *Endeavour*. 'You poor sod,' observes Lewis, overhearing the revelation. We see Morse and Adele together in several Oxford settings – driving under the 'Bridge of Sighs', down New College Lane, and walking by the River Cherwell.

Anna Calder-Marshall, as Jane Robson

Amanda Hillwood, as Dr Grayling Russell, with Morse

Morse is hit hardest when Susan Fallon (Joanna David), to whom he was once engaged, eventually commits suicide after helping her terminally ill husband end his life (*Dead on Time*). The River Cherwell is again the setting for a poignant talk, by the blue gates near the bridge over Holywell Stream at Magdalen College and through the water meadows.

Morse suffers mild shock rather than the pangs of love when pathologist Dr Grayling Russell (Amanda Hillwood) arrives to examine the battered body of Sir Julius Hanbury (Michael Godley) in *Ghost in the Machine*. She is amused, then irritated by his patronizing attitude, but their mutual attraction grows. They meet over dead bodies – at the canal at Thrupp and in Pembroke College (the Arnold College of *Deceived by Flight*) – but when they finally get to dance together, Morse is called away to Oxford's Westgate car park (*The Secret of Bay 5B*) to view another corpse.

Lost love

'Losing a woman like that – I might turn a bit sour myself,' muses Lewis after finding out that Morse had once been engaged to Susan Fallon in *Dead on Time*.

He flirts on Exeter College lawn with the mendacious Claire Osborne (Vivienne Ritchie) in *The Way Through the Woods*, and tries to rekindle romance with Jane Robson (Anna Calder-Marshall) as he helps push her wheelchair-bound father across Magdalen Bridge and into the Botanic Garden in *The Settling of the Sun*. Morse, attracted by prison governor Hilary Stevens (Diana Quick) in *Absolute Conviction*, has intense conversations with her in a moodily lit Radcliffe Square, but their lives are too diverse. The same goes for Helen Field (Geraldine James), with whom he talks in Blackwell's bookshop in *Who Killed Harry Field?*

Judy Loe, as Adele Cecil, with Morse

HEART OF THE MYSTERY

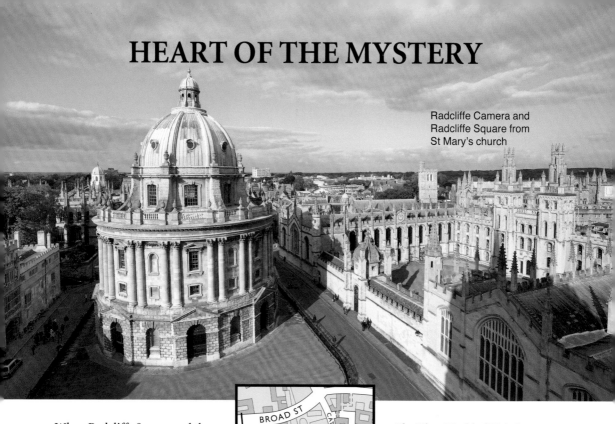

Radcliffe Camera and
Radcliffe Square from
St Mary's church

When Radcliffe Square and the
great domed Radcliffe Camera
are shown in the opening shots,
it's certain that the investigations
will be focused on the University,
where an undergraduate, fellow
or even the master of a college is
involved in fraud, duplicity or
murder. Radcliffe Square lies
close to Broad Street and Turl Street, in the
heart of Oxford. The area sets the scene for
many Morse mysteries.

Radcliffe Square

Radcliffe Square is surrounded by some of the
grandest buildings in the world, with Brasenose
College to the west, All Souls College to the east
and the University Church of St Mary the Virgin
to the south. Radcliffe Camera, one of Oxford's
best known landmarks, lies at the centre of the
cobbled square. Built between 1737 and 1749,
it is now used as the principal reading room of
the Bodleian Library.

It is from the tall tower of St Mary's that we
get a view over the area and the imposing outline
of All Souls College in the opening scenes of

*The Silent World of Nicholas
Quinn.* Another aerial view appears
dramatically in *Twilight
of the Gods* when the Radcliffe
Camera is shown from the vantage
point of rich villain Andrew
Baydon's (Robert Hardy)
helicopter, clattering overhead.

Morse walks piano teacher Anne Staveley
(Gemma Jones) through Radcliffe Square as they
set out to her Jericho home after choir practice in
The Dead of Jericho. And it is in Radcliffe Square,
more dramatically, that the blood-stained bicycle
belonging to the unpleasant Ted Brooks (Anthony
Haygarth) in *The Daughters of Cain* is found.
Perhaps the most atmospheric shots of this area
show Morse in conversation with prison governor
Hilary Stevens in *Absolute Conviction.*

The Settling of the Sun opens with hopeful
summer-school students disembarking from
a coach that is parked between the Radcliffe
Camera and Brasenose College. And Morse
somehow manages to drive his red Jaguar 2.4
through this normally pedestrianized square in
The Way Through the Woods. This central point in
Oxford also features in *Last Bus to Woodstock* and
The Last Enemy.

Radcliffe Camera

The great dominating rotunda, built to house the valuable library of Dr John Radcliffe, medical advisor to Queen Anne and great benefactor to Oxford, was designed by architect James Gibbs. Fellow architect Nicholas Hawksmoor first mooted the idea of a circular building, but he died before work on the Camera (from the Latin word for a room) started. The Radcliffe book collection is now stored in the Radcliffe Science Library in Parks Road.

Brasenose College

Brasenose, along with Oriel College (see page 19), is one of the colleges most used for location shots in the *Inspector Morse* television series. It is the Lonsdale College of *The Silent World of Nicholas Quinn*; in this episode, Morse interviews the murderous Christopher Roope (Anthony Smee) here, and Lewis walks through the tiny Chapel Quad (known as the 'Deer Park') and Old Quad into Radcliffe Square.

In *Death is Now My Neighbour*, aspiring Denis Cornford (Roger Allam) rushes out of a car and

Brasenose gatehouse

into Brasenose College (Lonsdale) gatehouse, late for an important meeting with the men who will decide if he is to be the college's next master. Later in the same episode, Morse and Lewis walk out of Brasenose into lamp-lit Radcliffe Square.

Sir John Gielgud, playing the part of Lord Hinksey, a malicious university chancellor, rehearses his speech here in *Twilight of the Gods*, and Brasenose is the setting for the summer school organized by Jane Robson in *The Settling of the Sun*. In *The Last Enemy*, Brasenose becomes Beaumont College and Morse and Carol Sharp (Sian Thomas) visit 'Gerties', the college buttery.

Filming in Radcliffe Square

'Brazen nose'

Founded in 1509, Brasenose is said to take its name from the brazen (bronze) nose-shaped door knocker, which can be seen hanging in the dining hall. Here too are portraits of Lord Runcie, former Archbishop of Canterbury, and Sir William Golding, writer and Nobel prize-winner.

HEART OF THE MYSTERY

Old Schools Quadrangle and Bodleian Library

Morse is often to be seen walking across the Old Schools Quadrangle outside the Bodleian Library buildings, north of Radcliffe Square. The Bodleian, the main research library for the University, is one of the most famous libraries in the world, holding a copy of every book published in Britain. The main part of the library is entered through the Old Schools Quadrangle, with the Tower of the Five Orders of Architecture (Tuscan, Doric, Ionic, Corinthian and Composite) at one end and Thomas Bodley's Proscholium, the

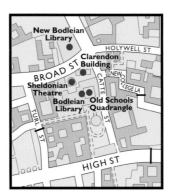

entrance to the library, at the other. The statue in front of the Proscholium is of the third Earl of Pembroke, University Chancellor from 1617 to 1630.

In *The Settling of the Sun*, foreshadowing the dramatic action to follow, Morse visits an art exhibition in the Bodleian Library featuring 'Images of Christ'. The programme he holds, as he walks across the Old Schools Quadrangle, past the statue of the Earl of Pembroke, shows a stigmata, signifying crucifixion. Reforming prison governor Hilary Stevens (*Absolute Conviction*) walks through the quadrangle, too, to meet Morse. There is more drama here in *Twilight of the Gods*, when Morse and Lewis find a revolver hidden behind some books in a Bodleian reading room. It was the gun used to shoot one of Morse's heroines, opera singer Gwladys Probert (Sheila Gish). A Bodleian reading room is also where American historian, Dr Millie Van Buren (Lisa Eichhorn), author of a book on the 19th-century Oxford canal murders, goes to do some research, and sees Morse's temporary assistant PC Adrian Kershaw (Matthew Finney) doing his own sleuthing in *The Wench is Dead*.

Books and more books

The Bodleian's immense collection cannot be housed in one space. Bodleian buildings include Duke Humfrey's Library above the Divinity School, the Old Schools Quadrangle, the Radcliffe Camera, the New Bodleian and the Clarendon Building in nearby Broad Street.

Entrance to the Bodleian Library

John Gielgud, as Lord Hinksey, in *Twilight of the Gods*

Sheldonian Theatre

The Sheldonian, designed by Christopher Wren, is used as a concert and lecture hall, and for formal university ceremonies such as Encaenia, when honorary degrees are conferred. The building is named for Gilbert Sheldon, Archbishop of Canterbury and University Chancellor in the latter half of the 17th century. Inside you'll see the chancellor's throne in a prominent position in the gilded auditorium with its extraordinary painted ceiling.

Morse, passionate about music, enjoyed concerts at the Sheldonian. In *Dead on Time,* one of the saddest episodes, he is shocked to meet his old love and one-time fiancée, Susan Fallon. After the violent death of her brilliant but fatally ill husband, Morse takes her to a concert at the Sheldonian, where her favourite Schubert is played. The theatre and its impressive quadrangle feature briefly in *Last Seen Wearing* and *The Last Enemy*, where Morse and Lewis discuss the case. It is seen more closely inside and out in *Twilight of the Gods*, as witnesses to the dramatic shooting of opera diva Gwladys Probert are detained for questioning. The colourful Miss Probert, taking part in Encaenia, is hit as she paces in procession with Lord Hinksey through the Sheldonian quadrangle – but was she really the target?

Stone heads outside the Sheldonian Theatre

Bearded guardians

Tourists stop to examine the semicircle of extraordinary carved stone heads, bearded and gazing serenely across the road, on the Broad Street side of the Sheldonian Theatre. The heads are sculptor Michael Black's modern copies, based on the originals by Christopher Wren who, as a young architect, was commissioned to design the building they guard.

Sheldonian Quad

HEART OF THE MYSTERY

Broad Street

Aptly named Broad Street (often called simply 'The Broad') borders the buildings that form the north side of Radcliffe Square, including the Sheldonian, the Clarendon Building and the Museum of the History of Science.

Across the other side of the wide street is the main branch of Blackwell's bookshop, where Morse meets Helen Field in *Who Killed Harry Field?* Blackwell's music shop, another of his haunts, is not far away. Next door to the bookshop lies one of Morse's favourite pubs, the White Horse (see page 28).

The Tourist Information Centre in Broad Street stands on the former premises of Lloyds Bank, where Lewis interviewed the manager in *Last Seen Wearing*. Nearby is The Buttery, on the site of the now-closed Thornton's bookshop, the workplace of murdering Simon Harrison (Simon Hepworth) in the last television episode, *The Remorseful Day*.

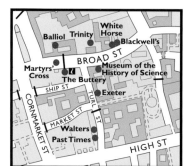

Trinity and Balliol

A few steps away from Blackwell's is the entrance to Trinity College, which features briefly in some episodes, including *The Wench is Dead*, where the college's gardens are the scene for a talk between historian Dr Millie Van Buren and Lewis's temporary replacement, PC Adrian Kershaw. Trinity has not one, but four, quadrangles and splendid gardens. The chapel contains carvings said to be by Grinling Gibbons.

Next door is Balliol College, one of Oxford's oldest colleges, founded by John Balliol in the late 13th century. Balliol is the setting for one of the most gruesome episodes, *The Day of the Devil*, where it transpires that the college bursar, Maugham Willowbank (Michael Culver), heads up a satanic cult.

Martyrs' cross

You'll see a cross marked in the road near the gates of Balliol College. This is where the Oxford Martyrs (Bishops Nicholas Ridley and Hugh Latimer and Archbishop Thomas Cranmer) were burnt at the stake for refusing to renounce their Protestant faith in the mid 16th century.

White Horse pub

Balliol College

Morse just before his fatal collapse in the grounds of Exeter College, *The Remorseful Day*

Turl Street

Opening into Broad Street across the road from Trinity College is Turl Street, an ancient and narrow street which contains long-established shops and the entrances to three colleges (Exeter, Jesus and Lincoln). Walters of Oxford, gentlemen's outfitters, is where Lewis made enquiries about the owner of a suit whose body was found in the canal in *The Last Enemy*, while another nearby shop was once Titles bookshop, where Morse, ever hopeful of good things to come, visits Claire Osborne, in *The Way Through the Woods*.

Exeter College

Exeter is the saddest location of all for Morse fans. It is on the lawn in Exeter's Front Quad that, in *The Remorseful Day*, the chief inspector collapses, as *In Paradisum* from Fauré's *Requiem* is played in the college chapel nearby; Morse had just listened to philandering surgeon Sir Lionel Phelps (T.P. McKenna) singing the *Libera Me* from the *Requiem*. The conductor is Morse music composer Barrington Pheloung. Morse is taken from here to hospital, where he later dies.

In happier days, Morse enjoyed a concert and a flirtation with Claire Osborne on Exeter's peaceful Fellows' Lawn (*The Way Through the Woods*). Exeter College features in *The Settling of the Sun*, when the Front Quad and the ancient former gatehouse, Palmer's Tower, are shown. The action ends, dramatically, in the richly decorated chapel. We see Lewis engaged in a chase here in

Blackwell's bookshop
The original shop, opened in 1879 by Benjamin Henry Blackwell, was so tiny that only three customers could squeeze in at a time. Now it is one of the largest bookshops in the world, with a basement (the Norrington Room) that has 5 kilometres (3 miles) of shelving.

Exeter College chapel

The Silent World of Nicholas Quinn. He ends up on the wall at the far end of the Fellows' Garden, which gives him a fine view of Radcliffe Square and of his quarry, the nasty Christopher Roope, far out of reach below.

HOLYWELL STREET AND NEW COLLEGE LANE

Holywell Street and New College Lane, lying just to the east of Broad Street, include some well-known Morse settings. The narrow, winding alleys leading between these streets, close to the medieval city wall, add to the atmosphere of mystery.

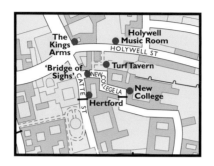

Holywell Music Room

The Holywell Music Room (1748), set back a little from Holywell Street, is believed to be the oldest concert hall in Europe. Handel and Haydn are among the many famous composers and musicians who have performed here. Morse applauds enthusiastically at a master class given here by forceful opera diva Gwladys Probert in *Twilight of the Gods.* Despite her unkind treatment of the young musician singing Mozart, he is moved to send the star red roses in anticipation of the concert she is to give later. But poor Gwladys is shot, the roses wilt and Morse finds himself heading a criminal investigation instead of concert-going. The Holywell Music Room is also where Morse talks to art expert Ian Matthews (Ronald Pickup) about forged paintings in *Who Killed Harry Field?*

Two Morse pubs

In this area you will find two of Morse's favourite pubs, the Turf Tavern and The Kings Arms (see pages 28–29). The Kings Arms, on the corner of Holywell Street and Parks Road, is a large and popular pub, with pavement tables. The Turf is one of the best known pubs in Oxford, but one of the hardest to find. You can reach it by following St Helen's Passage, a narrow alleyway off New College Lane, or from Bath Place, a cobbled lane off Holywell Street. Morse was fond of the wide selection of guest beers here.

Turf Tavern

Sheila Gish, as Gwladys Probert, in *Twilight of the Gods*

Hertford College and the 'Bridge of Sighs'

A few steps away from The Kings Arms, down Catte Street, is New College Lane, which is crossed by another famous Oxford landmark – the instantly recognizable 'Bridge of Sighs' or, as it is properly called, Hertford Bridge, which unites two buildings of Hertford College. We see Morse and Lewis walking under the bridge on their way to the Green Man (Turf Tavern) in *Service of All the Dead*. Hertford College itself is where Morse listens to Dr Bernard Crowther's (Anthony Bate) lecture in *Last Bus to Woodstock* and enjoys post-concert drinks on the lawn with old flame Susan Fallon in *Dead on Time*.

The name's the same
Both New College (founded 1379) and Oriel (1326) were originally named for the Virgin Mary. It is thought that Oriel received its present name because it was built on the site of a former property known as 'L'Oriole', while New College was so called to avoid confusion with the first 'House of the Blessed Virgin Mary'. In *The Wolvercote Tongue*, tour guide Cedric Downes forgets this fact, to the malicious glee of know-all tourist Janet Roscoe.

New College

New College, in New College Lane, is one of Oxford's grandest colleges. It is the main location in *Fat Chance*, where it is called St Saviour's. A group of clergymen here oppose the ordination of women and Morse comments 'I reckon we're seeing an extremely Oxford view of things, Lewis.' Hilary Dobson (Maggie O'Neill), finally elected college chaplain, executes a perfect cartwheel in the Front Quad. There are also scenes in the beautiful cloisters and the magnificent chapel and ante-chapel, dominated by Epstein's powerful 1948 sculpture, *Lazarus*. The college is also the scene of the humiliation of tour guide Cedric Downes (Kenneth Cranham) by rude American Janet Roscoe (Mildred Shay) in *The Wolvercote Tongue* (see panel). Poor Morse is hounded by the tabloid press in *Happy Families* and it is by New College garden gates that two reporters mock him as he and his friend Professor Joshua Masterson (Ralph Nossek), expert on Eastern Europe, walk in the cloisters.

New College cloisters

CARFAX AND ST ALDATES

Carfax, the ancient heart of Oxford, is a busy crossroads where four roads, once leading in from the old city gates, meet. To the north is Cornmarket and to the south St Aldates, which goes down to Oxford police station and the river. Queen Street to the west leads to New Road, where you'll find Oxford Prison, and to the east is the High Street (see pages 14–17).

Carfax and Carfax Tower

At one time the site of a large market, Carfax still lies at the centre of city life. Carfax Tower, all that remains of the medieval city church of St Martin, stands at the north-west corner. Visitors who climb the 99 steps to the top of the tower are rewarded by a grand view of the Oxford skyline, a view used in some of the opening shots in the television series. Author Colin Dexter, who appears briefly in most of the episodes, is seen at Carfax in the guise of a drunken man in *Happy Families*. Morse and Lewis, on their way to interview Alfred Rydale (Andrew Ray), walk past him. We see Morse at Carfax again in *The Last Enemy*, as he finds a litter bin for an unwanted newspaper.

St Aldates

Just south of Carfax in St Aldates is the Town Hall. The old courtroom here is the setting for the historical trial of those wrongly convicted and hanged for the 1859 murder of Joanna Franks (Juliet Cowan) in *The Wench is Dead*.

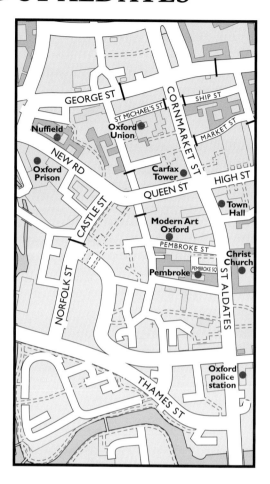

Colin Dexter being made up for his part in *Happy Families*

St Aldates is also where scheming nurse Wendy Hazlitt (Penny Downie) lives and paints in *Deadly Slumber*, and it is here that Morse visits her and spots a painting that gives away her relationship with the murderer.

Pembroke Street

Turn down Pembroke Street and you'll find Modern Art Oxford, a contemporary world-class gallery where Morse is to be found during his investigations in *Who Killed Harry Field?* Nearby is Pembroke Square, with its view across to the imposing Tom Tower of Christ Church College (see page 20), a shot we see in the rain-washed opening to *Last Bus to Woodstock*. Pembroke College itself is the Arnold College of *Deceived by Flight*, where we see Lewis in a new light as a handy all-rounder on the cricket field.

Oxford police station

At the bottom of St Aldates is Oxford police station. Filming took place here for scenes in several episodes, but most police station scenes, including those showing the offices and car park, were shot elsewhere. A plaque marking the link between Morse and the Thames Valley Police was erected here by the Inspector Morse Society and unveiled in 2006 by Colin Dexter. Two police dogs, named Morse and Lewis, joined the celebrations.

Cornmarket

This busy shopping street is where, in *The Last Enemy,* Morse and Lewis give chase to the terminally ill Professor Drysdale (Michael Aldridge), managing to collide with his bicycle and knock

him to the ground at the junction with Ship Street. Just off Cornmarket, in St Michael Street, are the Oxford Union buildings. It is here that Dr Julian Dear (David Neal), the first murder victim in *The Infernal Serpent*, was due to speak in a debate on environmental issues.

Nuffield College and Oxford Prison

Nuffield College in New Road is one of the locations for St Saviour's College of *Fat Chance*, along with New College, and it is the butt of a joke from smart copper Adrian Kershaw in *The Wench is Dead*. Nearby is Oxford Prison, the location for the hanging of the innocent boatmen in the same episode; it is now a tourist attraction.

Oxford police station

Nuffield College   Ship Street (below)

Pembroke College

Pembroke was founded in 1624 with the backing of the then university chancellor, William Herbert, Earl of Pembroke. One of its best known 'old boys' was lexicographer Samuel Johnson. Sadly, Pembroke is not normally open to visitors.

HIGH STREET

The High Street (often known locally as 'The High') is one of Oxford's grandest streets, a gently curving thoroughfare leading east from Carfax to Magdalen College and the Botanic Garden. Ancient passageways and lanes open off the street, connecting with Morse locations to both north and south. A good view of the High Street, from the top of Carfax Tower (see page 12), is shown in *Death is Now My Neighbour*, as Morse and Lewis drive down the street on their way to investigate the murder of blackmailing reporter Geoffrey Owens (Mark McGann).

Medieval lanes and the Covered Market

Not far from Carfax, across the road from the entrance to the Covered Market, lies Wheatsheaf Yard. Down this narrow alleyway you'll find Gill & Co. Ironmongers, where keys are checked in *The Dead of Jericho* and the goods are swept off display and smashed by disgruntled ex-employee John Sanders (Ian Sears) in *Last Bus to Woodstock*. Magpie Lane, leading to cobbled Merton Street, is the route that Morse and Lewis take as they walk together, pondering the possibilities in *Deadly Slumber*.

There's action of a less leisurely nature in *Absolute Conviction* when Lewis chases prisoner Charlie Bennett (Jim Broadbent) along Bear Lane, into the Alfred Street door of the tiny

Morse and Lewis in Magpie Lane

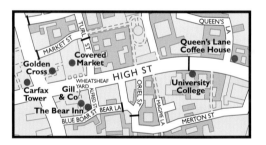

High Street from Carfax Tower

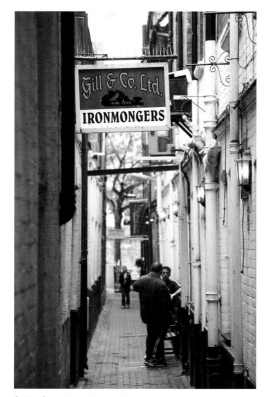
Gill & Co., Wheatsheaf Yard

Bear Inn (see page 29) and out again into Blue Boar Street, up narrow Wheatsheaf Yard and across the High Street into the crowded Covered Market. Morse parks his Jaguar and joins the chase, tripping heavily over a greengrocer's stall. He is helped to his feet by Bennett (who is on parole), and a cup of tea in the market's Brown's Café restores equilibrium.

The Covered Market and adjoining Golden Cross arcade feature also in *Greeks Bearing Gifts.* Maria Capparis (Elvira Poulianou), sister of Nicos, a murdered chef at a local Greek restaurant, gives interpreter Jocasta Georgiadis (Eve Adam) the slip here so that she can make a phone call.

A little further down from the Covered Market is Turl Street (see page 9), opening off the High Street to the north. Further down still, on the corner of the High Street and Queen's Lane, is the popular Queen's Lane Coffee House, part of which was once the Magna Gallery, which features in a couple of episodes. Brian Pierce (Philip McGough) takes paintings to the gallery to sell in *The Secret of Bay 5B,* while Christopher Roope (*The Silent World of Nicholas Quinn*), with Lewis in pursuit, emerges from the doorway to make his way down to the Botanic Garden.

University College

Three colleges open on to the High Street – University, The Queen's and Magdalen. It is in the chapel of University College, the oldest of the three, that we see Blanche Copley-Barnes (Barbara Leigh-Hunt), who has just murdered her husband Matthew (Geoffrey Palmer), the deeply unpleasant master of Beaufort College in *The Infernal Serpent*, threaten to throw herself from the lofty organ case as the choir sings below. Morse and Lewis persuade her to come down in the closing scenes.

Brown's Café, Covered Market

University College
'Univ' together with Balliol and Merton is one of the oldest colleges in Oxford, founded in the mid 13th century. Sadly, it is not open to members of the public, but you can look through the 17th-century gate-house into the Front Quad.

Covered Market
There has been a market here since 1772 when the stalls that cluttered Oxford streets were tidied onto one site. In those days there were at least 40 butchers' shops here but now you can buy anything from a new hat to fresh fruit and local cheese.

Magdalen College

Magdalen College (like its Cambridge counterpart pronounced 'maudlin') is every-thing an Oxford college should be. Ancient cloisters surround a perfectly mown lawn, there are well-kept gardens, historic stonework, heraldic figures and dozens of carved 'grotesques' gazing from the high walls of the centuries-old buildings. Visitors may walk through the grounds to admire the deer park, complete with grazing fallow deer, or follow the River Cherwell as it winds its way around the college land. Magdalen was founded on this site in 1458.

Morse finds himself visiting Magdalen to interview students and suspects, or to walk though the grounds. Perhaps the saddest occasion is when he talks to his old love, Susan Fallon, on the Holywell Stream bridge, walking through the water meadows with her in *Dead on Time*. We learn that they were once engaged to be married and presumably the end of their affair was the reason Morse left his studies. Poor Morse cannot believe that Susan was part of the murder conspiracy, so it is left to Lewis to destroy the answerphone tape that incriminates her, by throwing it into the River Cherwell here. A happier walk around the Cherwell is made with Adele Cecil in *Death is Now My Neighbour*.

In the first-ever episode, *The Dead of Jericho*, Morse walks through Magdalen cloisters to visit dysfunctional law student Ned Murdoch (Spencer Leigh). He passes a visitor in the cloisters – viewers' first glimpse of Colin Dexter. And the cloisters are where student Arabella Baydon (Rachael Weisz), daughter of evil Andrew Baydon, talks to her boyfriend in *Twilight of the Gods*, before going to her room on one of the staircases, to find it ransacked and a letter stolen.

We see the library of Magdalen College in *Greeks Bearing Gifts*, when Morse talks to Jerome Hogg (Richard Pearson) and a floodlit Magdalen is where he meets college fellow and Greek expert Randall Rees (Martin Jarvis) over dinner in the same episode. The chap in the porter's lodge as Morse leaves is – yes – Colin Dexter.

Morse makes his last visit to Magdalen in *The Remorseful Day* when, standing inside the college grounds just below Magdalen Bridge, he is rude to a tour guide.

Joanna David, as Susan Fallon, with Morse on Holywell Stream bridge

Magdalen College hall

Magdalen Bridge
This bridge, spanning the Cherwell between Magdalen College and the Botanic Garden, is where an incriminating cassette tape is thrown into the water by George Henderson (George Irving) in *The Secret of Bay 5B*.

Magdalen Bridge and Magdalen Tower

Wishful thinking
On finding dead journalist Neville Grimshaw in *Twilight of the Gods*, Morse remarks, 'It would be nice to enjoy the Isis [Oxford-speak for the River Thames] now and then, instead of always having to drag bodies out of it.'

Botanic Garden

Morse is not known for his love of horticulture, although the daylight shots of the garden surrounding his flat (actually located at Castlebar Park, Ealing) are impressive. However, he finds himself helping old friend, the nervous Jane Robson, to push her father, the Revd Robson (Llewellyn Rees) in his wheelchair over Magdalen Bridge and into the Botanic Garden in *The Settling of the Sun*. This is the oldest botanic garden in Britain where plants are grown for conservation, academic research and reference reasons. But it is beautifully laid out and there are well-filled glasshouses where the Revd Robson, tortured by memories of the past, wakes from an uneasy sleep and attacks one of the gardeners.

The Botanic Garden is the unlikely conclusion of a convoluted chase where Lewis, hot on

Botanic Garden

the heels of Christopher Roope in *The Silent World of Nicholas Quinn*, manages to follow him from Brasenose College, through Radcliffe Square and Exeter College, through St Edmund Hall, into the High Street and then into the Botanic Garden where Roope meets Dr Bartlett (Clive Swift), leaving Lewis looking foolish.

ORIEL SQUARE

Oriel Square, with brightly painted 18th-century houses fronting its eastern boundary, is a place to pause between the grandeur of the High Street and the charm of cobbled Merton Street. Oriel College gatehouse opens onto the square and the entrance to Corpus Christi College is on the square's southern edge. Closed to vehicles during the day, with space to film, it is featured in several episodes.

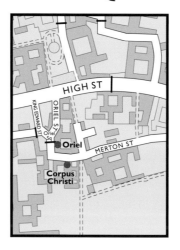

(Fiona Mollison), wife of philandering headmaster Donald Phillipson (Peter McEnery), walk through these gates in *Last Seen Wearing*, while Morse and Lewis linger outside them, talking things through in *Second Time Around*.

In reality, vehicles cannot access Oriel Square during the day, but Morse and Lewis manage to drive through it in *Absolute Conviction* when Lewis spots prisoner Charlie Bennett. Oriel Square is also where Blanche Copley-Barnes, unhappy wife of the deeply unpleasant master of Beaufort College (Merton in this case), tries to talk to gardener Phil Hopkirk (Ian Brimble) in *The Infernal Serpent*.

The square

The gate by which visitors exit Christ Church (see page 20) is in the south-western corner of Oriel Square. Morse and Sheila Phillipson

Gate into Oriel Square from Christ Church

Morse in Oriel's dining hall

Oriel College front quad

Oriel College

Oriel, founded in 1326, but largely rebuilt in the late 17th century, is the location for key scenes in many episodes. It is the Lonsdale College of *The Silent World of Nicholas Quinn*. In this episode, Oriel's dining hall is used as the setting for a reception for the Sheik of Al-jamara (Saul Reichlin), during which the deaf and ill-fated Nicholas Quinn (Phil Nice) lip-reads the words that were to lead to his death. The Front Quad is also shown, and Morse walks through St Mary's Quad, talking to the dean.

Oriel's dining hall is used again in *The Settling of the Sun* and it is here that Sir John Gielgud, as the autocratic university chancellor Lord Hinksey, makes a cleverly snide speech to his guests in *Twilight of the Gods.*

The action in *Ghost in the Machine* mostly takes place outside Oxford, but college scenes where the fellows are meeting to choose a new master were filmed at Oriel – this time named Courtenay College. The funeral service of environmentalist Dr Julian Dear, attacked and killed in *The Infernal Serpent*, takes place in Oriel College chapel, with a good shot of Morse creator Colin Dexter in the congregation, sitting next to the master's wife. Morse visits Oriel several times

Mark of distinction

One of the most distinctive features of Oriel College is the carving of the words 'Regnante Carolo' on the portico opposite the entrance gate in the Front Quad, marking its completion during the reign of Charles I (1625–49). These can be seen quite clearly in many shots of the Front Quad.

to question student Jane Folley (Carol Starks) during his enquiries concerning the murder of her boyfriend's father in *Deadly Slumber*.

Poor Shelly Cornford (Holley Chant), newly married to one of the two contenders for the post of master of Lonsdale, falls down the stairs to her death in Oriel in *Death is Now My Neighbour*, where scenes are shot in the quads, hall and chapel. Watch out for Colin Dexter saying Latin grace in the dining hall.

Corpus Christi

One of the smallest colleges in Oxford, Corpus Christi in Merton Street was founded in 1517. Its beautiful 16th- and 18th-century buildings retain many original features. Corpus Christi is one of the locations used for the Beaumont College of *The Last Enemy* (the other is Brasenose), where Morse and Carol Sharp walk in the cloisters. We also see the croquet lawn. What we don't see is the distinctive pelican-topped sundial in the Front Quad.

Corpus Christi cloisters

CHRIST CHURCH
AND MERTON COLLEGE

Christ Church, one of the grandest colleges in Oxford, and Merton, one of the oldest, stand close to each other, each overlooking Christ Church Meadow, which runs down to the river. This is idyllic Oxford: ancient towers, spires, cattle-filled meadows and rowing teams practising on the water. But, in the Oxford of Chief Inspector Morse, villainy knows no bounds.

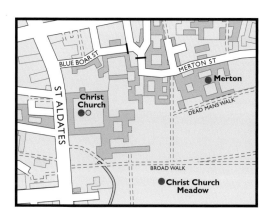

Christ Church

'The House', as Christ Church is often known (its second founder, Henry VIII, named it 'The House of Christ in Oxford'), was first founded by Cardinal Wolsey in 1524 as Cardinal College. But when the prelate fell from grace, the king stepped in and made the college his own. It is unique in that its college chapel serves as the Anglican cathedral for the city of Oxford.

Christ Church is the Wolsey College of *The Daughters of Cain*, where the unpleasant Ted Brooks, whose body is found in the river, had been a scout (college servant). The interior of the library is shown in *Last Seen Wearing* when Morse goes to interview Sheila Phillipson, wife of the headmaster of the exclusive boarding school from which schoolgirl Valerie Craven (Melissa Simmonds) has absconded. Morse is ushered into the library again in *Deadly Slumber* to interview student John Brewster (Jason Durr).

Christ Church's magnificent Tom Quad, so-called for 'Great Tom', the bell that still tolls 101 strokes at 9.05 each evening in honour of the college's 100 original students and one other who joined in 1663, is the largest quad in Oxford.

Speaking first

Morse creator Colin Dexter, who appears, Hitchcock-like, in many of the episodes, has his first speaking role in *Deadly Slumber* when he ushers Morse, anxious to interview student John Brewster, into Christ Church library and utters the words 'Mr Brewster'.

Morse and Lewis walk from the library, through Peckwater Quad and into Tom Quad as they make their enquiries in *Who Killed Harry Field?* Tom Quad is shown again in *The Daughters of Cain* as the detectives try to unravel the relationship of drug-dealing college scout Ted Brooks with murdered college fellow Felix McClure (Bernard Brown). The quad is also the location for celebratory drinks in *Twilight of the Gods*. Christ Church Picture Gallery is where Morse joins art forger Harry Field senior (Freddie Jones) before meeting Lewis and strolling back into Tom Quad.

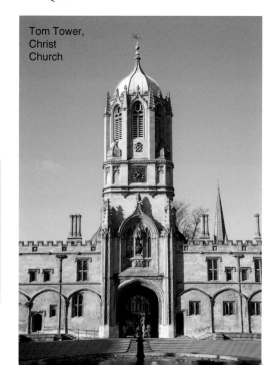

Tom Tower, Christ Church

Broad Walk

Many visitors enjoy walking through Christ Church Meadow and this is what Mari Probert (Caroline Berry), younger sister of opera singer Gwladys Probert, does in *Twilight of the Gods*, when she strolls along Broad Walk with her boyfriend.

Merton College

Above Merton's gatehouse on Merton Street is a carved panel which shows beasts, flowers and trees and the college's founder, Walter de Merton, together with St John the Baptist. This recognizes that the medieval church of St John the Baptist was razed to make way for the college, founded in the late 13th century.

Merton is the setting for one of the darkest episodes, *The Infernal Serpent*, in which it becomes Beaufort College. Long-hidden evil slowly comes to light as the master, Matthew Copley-Barnes, is revealed to have abused a child in his care. His past returns to haunt him and a

Morse and Milton
Morse winds up *The Infernal Serpent* by quoting Milton (*Paradise Lost, Book One*) to a long-suffering Lewis, as they leave the college: 'The Infernal Serpent, he it was whose guile, stirred up with envy and revenge, deceived the mother of mankind …'.

series of bizarre incidents takes place, culminating in his violent death. The earlier death of environmentalist Dr Julian Dear, mistaken for the master on a dark and rainy night, is also investigated by Morse and Lewis.

Morse visits Merton College in *Service of All the Dead* to talk to the Archdeacon about murdered vicar Lionel Pawlen (John Normington). They walk across the Front Quad into tiny Mob Quad, the oldest quadrangle in Oxford. They pass a man and a woman with a bicycle – the man is Colin Dexter.

Geoffrey Palmer, as Matthew Copley-Barnes, in Merton College

ST GILES

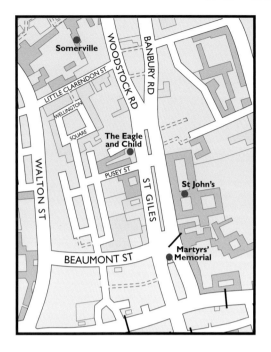

St Giles

Just a few minutes from the city centre is St Giles, a wide tree-lined avenue, which divides into Woodstock Road and Banbury Road to the north. The elegant street is named after the 12th-century church of St Giles, squeezed into a narrow piece of land between the roads above the city's war memorial. Morse often sweeps along St Giles behind the wheel of his red Jaguar.

Martyrs' Memorial

The tall monument at the south end of St Giles is the Martyrs' Memorial, dedicated to bishops Nicholas Ridley and Hugh Latimer and Arch-bishop Thomas Cranmer. It was erected in 1841, almost 300 years after the three churchmen were burnt to death for refusing to recant their Protestant faith. Cranmer faces north, holding his Bible, Ridley gazes eastwards and Latimer faces westwards, arms crossed and head bowed. Harassed courier Sheila Williams (Roberta Taylor) gives a brief description of the memorial in *The Wolvercote Tongue*, and later in the same episode tour guide Cedric Downes, standing on its steps to speak to his group, is humiliated by know-it-all American Janet Roscoe.

Tour group at the Martyrs' Memorial

The Eagle and Child

The Eagle and Child

The Eagle and Child pub (see page 29) in
St Giles, known locally as 'The Bird and Baby',
is featured in *Second Time Around* and *The
Way Through the Woods.*

Little Clarendon Street

Little Clarendon Street, with its interesting mix
of shops, cafés and restaurants, opens off
Woodstock Road, just north of St Giles, leading towards the Jericho area (see page 25). It is
in Little Clarendon Street that Denis Cornford,
aspiring master of Lonsdale, buys his young
wife, the glamorous Shelly, a new outfit for the
college feast in *Death is Now My Neighbour.* Just
around the corner in Wellington Square is the
Department of Criminology of the University
Law School where the clever PC Adrian Kershaw
digs out ancient evidence about the Oxford Canal
murder in *The Wench is Dead.*

Little Clarendon Street

No regrets?

Oxford's richest college, St John's, opens
off St Giles. Although the college is not a
location used in the television series, we
learn from Colin Dexter's book, *The Riddle
of the Third Mile* (televised as *The Last
Enemy*), that Morse was an undergraduate
at St John's, failing to complete his degree.
In *The Last Enemy* he says to his boss, Chief
Superintendent Strange (James Grout),
'Look, Sir, I was at Oxford with half the
senior men of the civil service.' 'And that's
where you learnt to behave so badly,' retorts
Strange. This is the television episode in
which Morse reveals to the terminally ill
Professor Drysdale that his university work
went to pieces because of a woman.

Radcliffe Infirmary

Many of the episodes show the exterior of the
Radcliffe Infirmary, next to Somerville College in
Woodstock Road. The infirmary, Oxford's first
hospital, opened in 1770 and closed in early 2007.
It is now used by the University, in the orginal
buildings. The infirmary was funded with money
from the will of John Radcliffe (1650–1714),
Queen Anne's physician, as was the Radcliffe
Camera in the centre of the city and the Radcliffe
Observatory in the grounds of Green College in
Woodstock Road. The Observatory is seen in *The
Silent World of Nicholas Quinn* and, as a back-
ground shot, in *The Dead of Jericho.*

Learned past

Although Morse is identified by Colin
Dexter in a 1983 book as a former St John's
College undergraduate, he is referred to
as an 'old Lonsdale man' in *Deceived by
Flight*, when we are told his nickname
was 'Pagan' and that he shared digs in St
John's Road with Anthony Donn (Daniel
Massey), an old Arnold College man, later,
alas, a murder victim.

BEAUMONT STREET

This pleasant street houses the Randolph Hotel and an internationally renowned museum, and leads to one of Oxford's least known colleges.

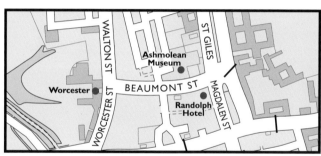

Randolph Hotel

The Randolph Hotel opened in 1866 and it remains Oxford's grandest and best known hotel. With its Morse Bar and commemorative plaque from the Inspector Morse Society, it is a favourite attraction for Morse fans. It played host to most of the cast and crew during filming in Oxford. It features in *The Wolvercote Tongue* (where Colin Dexter and writer of this episode Julian Mitchell can be spotted sitting in the hotel bar) and where American tourist Laura Poindexter (Christine Norden) dies of a heart attack in her room. Morse's last love, Adele Cecil, takes a civilized tea here with Chief Superintendent Strange in *The Wench is Dead* and it provides the setting for a dinner for the unpleasant Harrison family in *The Remorseful Day*. It's the obvious place for journalist Sylvie Maxton (Cheryl Campbell) to stay and talk to Morse in *The Infernal Serpent*, while Detective Chief Inspector Patrick Dawson (Kenneth Colley) and his wife Catherine (Ann Bell) stayed here during investigations into the past in *Second Time Around*.

Ashmolean Museum

This world-class museum opened in Broad Street in 1683, moving to its neo-classical home in Beaumont Street in 1845. A £61 million redevelopment began in 2007, doubling the display space. One of the most famous exhibits is the Alfred Jewel, an Anglo-Saxon gold and rock crystal gem, and it may be this on which Colin Dexter based the jewelled Saxon artefact in his book *The Jewel That Was Ours*. Screenwriter Julian Mitchell turned the story into the television episode *The Wolvercote Tongue*, where the pin that fits into an ancient buckle, brought back to the museum by Americans Laura and Eddie Poindexter (Robert Arden), disappears.

Worcester College

Worcester College, at the end of Beaumont Street, has 26 acres of garden with a lake, a row of 15th-century cottages and grand 18th-century buildings. We see naive student Angie Hartman (Holly Aird) in the Front Quad, with the ancient cottages behind her as she talks to Dr Bernard Crowther and her tutor, Peter Newlove (Paul Geoffrey), in *Last Bus to Woodstock*. In later scenes we see the college's lake and gardens. Worcester College library is shown in *The Sins of the Fathers*.

Morse Bar, Randolph Hotel

Worcester College

JERICHO

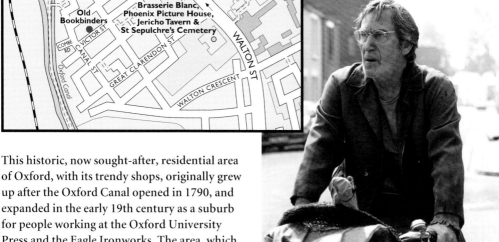

This historic, now sought-after, residential area of Oxford, with its trendy shops, originally grew up after the Oxford Canal opened in 1790, and expanded in the early 19th century as a suburb for people working at the Oxford University Press and the Eagle Ironworks. The area, which lies just north-west of the city centre, provides the main setting for the first television adaptation, *The Dead of Jericho*.

Patrick Troughton, as George Jackson, in *The Dead of Jericho*

Jericho settings

Morse, who sings in the same choir as piano teacher Anne Staveley, develops romantic hopes in her direction in *The Dead of Jericho*. He walks her home to 'Canal Reach' – in reality Combe Road off Canal Street. His hopes are tragically dashed when she is found hanged. Later we see her unpleasant neighbour George Jackson (Patrick Troughton) cycling along Walton Street, after picking up his blackmail money.

The Bookbinders Arms (now the Old Bookbinders; see page 29) in Victor Street (see page 28) features several times in *The Dead of Jericho*. The rather bleak interior of the pub was filmed elsewhere. Another Jericho pub is shown in *The Silent World of Nicholas Quinn*, when Morse, disappointed that his hopes of seeing *Last Tango in Paris* at the Studio 2 cinema are dashed,

Team work

It is in *The Dead of Jericho* that Morse and Lewis first become a team, as Morse, upset that Anne Staveley has been hanged, muscles in on the investigation and appropriates Lewis as his sergeant.

because it has come to the end of its run and is replaced by *101 Dalmatians*, retires to The Jericho Tavern, near the cinema in Walton Street. That cinema, now called the Phoenix Picture House, figures largely in the plot.

We visit Jericho again in *Death is Now My Neighbour* when blackmailing reporter and murder victim Geoffrey Owens lunches a girl-friend at Le Petit Blanc (now Brasserie Blanc) in Walton Street – something he would have found difficult if his only income had been a local newspaper reporter's salary.

St Sepulchre's Cemetery

This peaceful Victorian burial ground, reached from Walton Street, is where the unnamed Oxford Canal murder victim would have been buried in *The Wench is Dead*.

Combe Road, Jericho

PARKS ROAD

Named for the University Parks, which are bounded on their eastern edge by the River Cherwell, Parks Road leads from Broad Street past the museums that feature in *The Daughters of Cain*. Also in Parks Road, nearer the city centre, is Wadham College, where screenwriter Julian Mitchell, who wrote several episodes, was at one time an undergraduate.

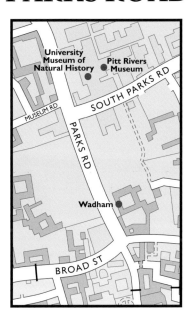

Wadham College

Wadham, which features in three *Inspector Morse* episodes, was built by a redoubtable woman, Dorothy Wadham, who organized its construction, drew up statutes, appointed all members and engaged the servants. Her husband Nicholas, who is honoured as co-founder, died before their intention of building an Oxford college could be carried out. Although Dorothy never left her West Country home to see what she had brought into being in 1613, she controlled all college business until her death in 1618. There are statues of Dorothy and Nicholas together with one of King James I, in Wadham's Front Quad.

The Libertine

Morse was interested in a famous – or rather infamous – and troubled alumnus of Wadham, 17th-century undergraduate John Wilmot, the licentious second Earl of Rochester, wit, lyricist and poet, most of whose work was obscene and pornographic. He died at the age of 33 in 1680 and his dissolute life has been recorded in the 2005 film *The Libertine*. In *Last Bus to Woodstock*, Morse joins undergraduate Angie Hartman at a lecture given by Dr Bernard Crowther on the life and work of Wilmot. Colin Dexter can be spotted in the audience too.

It is in Wadham's Front Quad that Morse meets art history expert Ian Matthews in *Who Killed Harry Field?* Sharp-eyed viewers will note a familiar face among a group of people nearby – Colin Dexter in the frame again. Wadham is where American historian Dr Millie Van Buren stays while in Oxford, promoting her book on the 1859 Oxford canal murders in *The Wench is Dead*. Morse, who is suddenly taken seriously ill, reads the book while in hospital and decides she's got it all wrong. We see him and Dr Van Buren walking together out of Wadham's Front Quad and towards Trinity College gates on Parks Road. In *The Daughters of Cain*, an episode written by Julian Mitchell, the Front Quad is used as the location for a reception.

Wadham College

Morse and Lewis in the University Museum, *The Daughters of Cain*

Gates to Trinity College, Parks Road

University museums

You can't miss the great dinosaur footprints across the lawn in front of the University Museum of Natural History. Once inside this light and airy Victorian Gothic building, you must, as Morse did, walk past great dinosaur skeletons to reach the Pitt Rivers Museum, which is featured in *The Daughters of Cain*.

More than half a million objects are displayed in the Pitt Rivers, including a wide-bladed ceremonial knife, which was given in 1919 to Bishop May by Zeta III, paramount chief of northern Rhodesia. That knife, no longer in its original case upstairs, but displayed near the entrance, was used as the murder weapon, killing both college fellow Felix McClure and unpleasant drug-dealing Ted Brooks. Morse fans will remember the clever twist when the knife appears to have been stolen several days after it was actually taken. The Pitt Rivers contains masks, weapons, textiles, currency, musical instruments, tools, fetishes, jewellery and a lot more besides,

including objects collected during Captain James Cook's expedition to the South Pacific. The core of the collection was donated by Lt. Gen. Augustus Henry Lane Fox Pitt Rivers in 1884.

MORSE'S PUBS

Morse is a thinker, his thought processes boosted by music, crossword-solving and a good pint. 'I need a beer, Lewis,' is the signal for some serious intellectual effort and the probability that Morse's long-suffering sergeant will be paying the price of the pint that provides the inspiration. Several pubs in Oxford and just outside the city are used as locations for these thinking and drinking sessions.

White Horse

The White Horse is sandwiched between two branches of Blackwell's bookshop in Broad Street. The small 18th-century timber-framed building is full of character and atmosphere. Morse and Lewis arrive too late for service as they investigate the disappearance of a schoolgirl in *Last Seen Wearing*. But Morse enjoys a pint here with soon-to-be-murdered Anne Staveley in *The Dead of Jericho*. It is here that he leaves lively pathologist Dr Grayling Russell when he dashes outside to pursue his enquiries with another woman in *The Secret of Bay 5B*.

Turf Tavern

It can be a bit of a challenge to find the Turf, tucked away down St Helen's Passage, off New College Lane. It started life as a malt house, becoming a cider house in 1775 and an inn, The

Gemma Jones, as Anne Staveley, with Morse in the White Horse

Sign outside the Turf Tavern

Spotted Cow, at the end of the 18th century. It took its present name in 1847 and is enjoyed by tourists and students alike. Morse and Lewis chat here in *The Settling of the Sun* as they investigate the murder of a Japanese summer-school student. In *Service of All the Dead*, Morse leaves without a beer after seeing Ruth Rawlinson (Angela Morant), whom he had hoped to take out to dinner, drinking with another man, murderer Harry Josephs (Maurice O'Connell).

The Kings Arms

Colin Dexter, a crossword fan like his fictional chief inspector, enjoys solving his puzzles in this old coaching inn on the corner of Holywell Street and Parks Road – they even supply a dictionary. The pub is the starting point for *Deadly Slumber*, where student Jane Foley is

The Kings Arms

uneasy about the mood of her boyfriend John Brewster. Later in this episode, John's father is found murdered in his garage. And The Kings Arms is where Morse and Lewis drink in *The Secret of Bay 5B*.

The Bear Inn

An extraordinary collection of neatly snipped-off ties, all labelled and catalogued, cover the walls of this tiny pub in Alfred Street, off the High Street. Lewis didn't get a chance to examine the collection when he pursued his quarry, prisoner Charlie Bennett, through the two small bars, in *Absolute Conviction*.

The Eagle and Child

Most famous for its association with 'The Inklings', a group of Oxford writers including J.R.R. Tolkien and C.S. Lewis, The Eagle and Child (or 'The Bird and Baby' as it is often called) in St Giles is the setting for a wine bar in *Second Time Around* and Morse and Lewis have an acrimonious discussion here in *The Way Through the Woods*.

Old Bookbinders

Those who drink at this characterful pub in Victor Street, Jericho, will know the interior scenes in *The Dead of Jericho*, showing a barn-like bar, were not filmed here. The pub opened as The Bookbinders Arms in the early 19th century, around the time the University Press moved to this part of Oxford.

Victoria Arms

The River Cherwell runs past the lawns of the Victoria Arms in Old Marston, and many customers arrive by punt or boat to enjoy the setting. Morse takes a punt up the river here with high-class call girl Kay Brooks (Amanda Ryan), while he pursues his investigations in *The Daughters of Cain*. He and Lewis visit the pub again in *Who Killed Harry Field?* and, sadly, on a cold wintry day in the last episode, *The Remorseful Day*. And here you'll find photographs of the filming pinned up over the bar and a plaque presented by the Inspector Morse Society.

Amanda Ryan, as Kay Brooks, with Morse, taking a punt to the Victoria Arms

AROUND OXFORD

With two rivers and a canal weaving their way around Oxford, it is not surprising that corpses are found floating in water in several episodes of *Inspector Morse*. Shallow graves in woodland are another favourite disposal spot for villains seeking to hide what they have done. Morse often needs to arm himself with a pint in order to think, and will travel a little way outside the city to find a pub that gives him the space to muse. He also has to visit a stately home at Woodstock.

The Boat Inn

Blenheim Palace and Woodstock

Blenheim Palace, in the village of Woodstock about 13 kilometres (8 miles) north-west of Oxford, was the creation of architects John Vanburgh and Nicholas Hawksmoor in the early 18th century, and the grounds were landscaped by Capability Brown in the 1760s. It is in these grounds that the body of blackmailer George Daley (Chris Fairbank) is found shot dead in *The Way Through the Woods*. Morse arrives at the scene and meets pathologist Dr Laura Hobson (Clare Holman) for the first time. There's a good view of Blenheim Park as Morse carries out his interviews. Woodstock is the village where the action happens in *Last Bus to Woodstock*, but the pub car park where Sylvia Kane (Jenny Jay) dies is actually a railway station in Surrey.

Wytham Woods

These ancient woods, belonging to Oxford University, occupy nearly 1,000 acres near the village of Wytham to the north-west of the city. They are the named backdrop for the action in *The Way Through the Woods*, but the filming actually took place near Dorking in Surrey. The woods are named again in *The Secret of Bay 5B* as a base for forest warden George Henderson. This time the filming was done in Berkshire woodland. However, the White Hart pub in the village of Wytham is shown when Henderson's scheming wife Rosemary (Mel Martin) stops outside to make a phone call.

Thrupp

This tiny canal-side hamlet, to the north of Oxford, with its rows of moored boats and basin, is where a young couple, losing control of their narrowboat and barging into the bank, find a headless body in *The Last Enemy*. Morse, suffering from toothache, dulls the pain at the Boat Inn here. One of Thrupp's pretty waterside cottages was home to Dr David Kerridge (Tenniel Evans), vice-master at Beaumont College in the same episode.

Thrupp canal basin

Wolvercote

The Trout Inn at Godstow, Lower Wolvercote, is often featured in the Morse television dramas. We see Morse and Lewis standing on the nearby bridge, just above Godstow weir, looking at the floodlit pub in *The Wolvercote Tongue*. The dramatic conclusion to that episode shows the 'tongue' – the missing pin from an antique buckle – recovered by a diver, raising his arm in Arthurian fashion straight up from the depths of the River Thames.

Godstow weir

Didcot Railway Centre

Tourist Howard Brown (Bill Reimbold) avoids more footslogging with his group around Oxford in *The Wolvercote Tongue* when he escapes alone to see some of the great collection of steam engines, wagons and coaches at this railway museum 16 kilometres (10 miles) to the south of the city. It's what Brown sees on the train on the way back that helps Morse and Lewis.

Old Marston

The church and the riverside Victoria Arms pub in Old Marston, to the north-east of the city, feature in several episodes. The Victoria Arms (see page 29) is the last Oxford pub that Morse visits (see panel) before his death.

Victoria Arms

Prophetic words

Morse is in a deeply reflective mood as he and Lewis sit drinking in the wintry garden at the Victoria Arms, Old Marston, in the final episode. The clue to the title of that episode and to its sad ending are in the lines he quotes from A.E. Houseman as he watches the sun fall in the west:

Ensanguining the skies
How heavily it dies
Into the west away;
Past touch and sight and sound
Not further to be found,
How hopeless under ground
Falls the remorseful day.

INFORMATION

Many of the colleges and other buildings shown in the *Inspector Morse* television dramas are open at certain times, generally in the afternoons. Some colleges may only be seen on an organized tour, and some are not open to the public. It is best to ring individual colleges to check before you visit. The university museums and other buildings such as the Sheldonian Theatre are also open to the public, but you should check opening times before your visit. The Radcliffe Camera is a reading room of the Bodleian Library and very rarely open to visitors.

Morse walking tours

Oxford Information Centre in Broad Street offers Saturday afternoon Inspector Morse Walking Tours. Contact them on 01865 686 441 or visit www.experienceoxfordshire.org for details.

Colleges featured in Inspector Morse episodes

Balliol College, Broad Street, p 8,
www.balliol.ox.ac.uk tel: 01865 277777
Brasenose College, Radcliffe Square, p 5,
www.bnc.ox.ac.uk tel: 01865 277830
Christ Church, St Aldates, p 20,
www.chch.ox.ac.uk tel: 01865 276150
Corpus Christi, Merton Street, p 19,
www.ccc.ox.ac.uk tel: 01865 276700
Exeter College, Turl Street, p 9,
www.exeter.ox.ac.uk tel: 01865 279600
Hertford College, Catte Street, p 11,
www.hertford.ox.ac.uk tel: 01865 279400
Magdalen College, Magdalen Street, p 16,
www.magd.ox.ac.uk tel: 01865 276000
Merton College, Merton Street, p 21,
www.merton.ox.ac.uk tel: 01865 276310
New College, New College Lane, p 11,
www.new.ox.ac.uk tel: 01865 279500
Nuffield College, New Road, p 13,
www.nuffield.ox.ac.uk tel: 01865 278500
Oriel College, Oriel Square, p 19
www.oriel.ox.ac.uk tel: 01865 276555
Pembroke College, Pembroke Square, p 12,
www.pmb.ox.ac.uk tel: 01865 276444
Trinity College, Broad Street, p 8,
www.trinity.ox.ac.uk tel: 01865 279900
University College, High Street, p 15,
www.univ.ox.ac.uk tel: 01865 276602
Wadham College, Parks Road, p 26,
www.wadham.ox.ac.uk tel: 01865 277900
Worcester College, Worcester Street, p 24,
www.worc.ox.ac.uk tel: 01865 278300

Museums and public buildings

Ashmolean Museum, Beaumont Street, p 24,
www.ashmolean.org tel: 01865 278112
Bodleian Library, Broad Street, p 6,
www.bodley.ox.ac.uk tel: 01865 277000
Botanic Garden, Rose Lane, p 17,
www.obga.ox.ac.uk tel: 01865 286690
Christ Church Picture Gallery, Oriel Square, p 20,
www.chch.ox.ac tel: 01865 276150
Modern Art Oxford, Pembroke Street, p 12,
www.modernartoxford.org.uk tel: 01865 722733
Pitt Rivers Museum, Parks Road, p 27,
www.prm.ox.ac.uk tel: 01865 270927
Sheldonian Theatre, Broad Street, p 7,
www.sheldon.ox.ac.uk tel: 01865 277299
University Museum of Natural History, Parks Road, p 27, www.oum.ox.ac.uk tel: 01865 272950

Oxford Information Centre

15–16 Broad Street
Oxford OX1 3AS
tel: 01865 686430
email: info@experienceoxfordshire.org
website:www.experienceoxfordshire.org